Little Pebble™

Celebrate Spring

Animals in Spring

by Kathryn Clay

CAPSTONE PRESS
a capstone imprint

Little Pebble is published by Capstone Press,
1710 Roe Crest Drive, North Mankato, Minnesota 56003
www.mycapstone.com

Library of Congress Cataloging-in-Publication Data
Clay, Kathryn, author.
  Animals in spring / by Kathryn Clay.
     pages cm.—(Little pebble. Celebrate spring)
  Audience: Ages 5–7.
  Audience: K to grade 3.
  Summary: "Simple nonfiction text and full-color photographs present animals in spring"—Provided by the publisher.
  Includes bibliographical references and index.
  ISBN 978-1-4914-8302-2 (library binding)—
  ISBN 978-1-4914-8306-0 (paperback)—
  ISBN 978-1-4914-8310-7 (ebook pdf)
  1. Animal behavior—Juvenile literature. 2. Animals—Juvenile literature. 3. Spring—Juvenile literature. I. Title.
   QL751.5.C555 2016
   591.5—dc23   2015023301

Editorial Credits
Erika L. Shores, editor; Juliette Peters and Ashlee Suker, designers;
Svetlana Zhurkin, media researcher; Katy LaVigne, production specialist

Photo Credits
Dreamstime: Saje, 13; iStockphoto: MRaust, 19; Shutterstock: AEPhotographic, 7, bluecrayola, 11 (inset), Cindy Underwood, 1, Dennis van de Water, 9, Edwin Butter, cover, Gucio_55, 17, Jiang Hongyan, 3, Kletr, 5, Matt Jeppson, 21, Matteo Photos, 11, Menno Schaefer, 15, USBFCO, back cover and throughout, Vasily Vishnevskiy, 7 (inset)

Table of Contents

Spring Is Here!

Animals are busy in spring.

They build nests.

They find food.

Babies Are Born

A duck finds sticks and leaves.

She makes a nest for her eggs.

Soon ducklings waddle.

They splash in ponds.

Frogs lay eggs.

Tadpoles hatch.

They grow into adult frogs.

Rabbits make grass nests.

Baby rabbits cuddle.

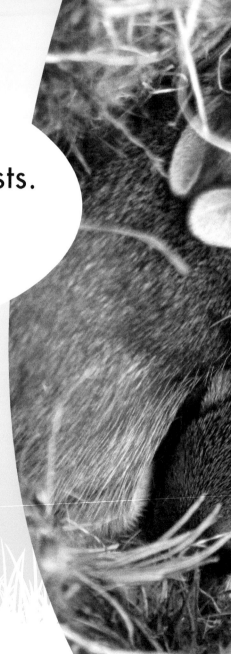

Fox pups yip.

Mothers bring back food.

Sleepy Animals Wake Up

Bats stretch their wings.

They look for food at night.

Bears leave their dens.

They find plants to eat.

Snakes lie on rocks.

The sun warms their bodies.

What do you do in spring?

Glossary

den—an animal home

hatch—to break out of an egg

nest—a home made by an animal for its young

tadpole—the life stage between egg and frog

Read More

DeGezelle, Terri. *Exploring Spring.* Exploring the Seasons. North Mankato, Minn.: Capstone Press, 2012.

Fogliano, Julie. *And Then It's Spring.* New York: Roaring Brook Press, 2012.

Ghigna, Charles. *I See Spring.* I See. Mankato, Minn.: Picture Window Books, 2012.

Internet Sites

FactHound offers a safe, fun way to find Internet sites related to this book. All of the sites on FactHound have been researched by our staff.

Here's all you do:
Visit *www.facthound.com*
Type in this code: 9781491483022

 Super-cool stuff! Check out projects, games and lots more at **www.capstonekids.com**

Index